Sisters, Brothers, and Disability

A *Family Album*

Lydia Gans

Fairview Press
Minneapolis

Published by Fairview Press, 2450 Riverside Avenue South, Minneapolis, MN 55454.

Library of Congress Cataloging-in-Publication Data
      Gans, Lydia, 1931–
         Sisters, brothers, and disability: a family album / Lydia Gans.
           p.   cm.
         Summary: Depicts twenty-six families raising children with special needs, with an emphasis on the interactions with other siblings.
         ISBN 1–57749–044–4 (pbk.: alk. paper)
         1. Handicapped children--United States--Family relationships--Case studies--Juvenile literature. 2. Handicapped children--United States--Social conditions--Case studies--Juvenile literature. 3. Brothers and sisters--United States--Case studies--juvenile literature. [1. Handicapped.] I. Title.
         HV888.5.G35   1997   97-24862
                                                 CIP
                                               AC

FIRST EDITION
First Printing: October 1997

Printed in the United States of America
01 00 99 98 97   7 6 5 4 3 2 1

Cover design: Laurie Duren
Photos: Lydia Gans

For a free current catalog of Fairview Press titles, please call 1-800-544-8207, or visit our web site at www.press.fairview.org.

CONTENTS

ACKNOWLEDGMENTS

I would like to say thank you:

To special friends Sue Hodges, who found time to give help and support in spite of a busy schedule, and to Marianne Miller, who read everything and asked good questions.

To Jo Ann Duprat, the nurse at Children's Hospital who cared for so many of these children, and to Louise Schneiders, a mother who became an activist for all children with special needs, for their helpful comments and suggestions.

To Kathy Simpson, director of education and disability programs for Planned Parenthood, and to Pam Steneberg, advocate with the Disability Rights and Education Fund, for their generosity in sharing their resources and information.

To Gene Gordon for his help and encouragement, and above all, for being here to share my pleasure in doing this work.

DEDICATION

To Ed Roberts

He was a good friend and an ardent fighter for independence

INTRODUCTION

This book could not have been written twenty-five years ago. In the United States, it is a relatively new concept that children with disabilities should live at home with their brothers and sisters, go to public school, and play with neighborhood children. Placing children with disabilities in institutions was accepted policy—indeed, it was required by law in most states—until this century. Segregation was a humane and progressive step compared to the days when a child with a disability would be kept out of sight and treated more like an animal than a human being. Although putting children in an institution was intended to isolate them from the rest of society, this represented a step forward by at least recognizing their humanity.

A child with a disability was not thought of as a person, but as a burden. A creative parent might have constructed some sort of mechanical gadget, perhaps a crutch or prosthetic limb, to help the youngster perform a particular task. But programs for special education, training, or therapy for physical or mental disabilities were rare. Only after World War I, when large numbers of young men with serious injuries tried to re-enter society, did communities begin to rehabilitate and integrate people with disabilities into the mainstream. Meanwhile, segregation of children with disabilities into special schools continued. It was not until 1973, nineteen years after Congress outlawed racial segregation in schools, that federal legislators declared that "separate but equal" for disabled children was no more fair or equal than it had been for black children. These laws were not very actively enforced, however. The Americans with Disabilities Act, passed in 1990, provided stronger regulations.

Today, placing children with special needs in institutions is abhorrent to most parents. More and more young people are being included in family and community activities, as well as in regular school classes and programs. Parents and educators are recognizing the value for both able-bodied and disabled children in learning and playing together. Everyone gains when children learn to get along with and appreciate others who are different.

In this book, you will meet twenty-six families—traditional nuclear, extended, and non-traditional families—raising children with special needs at home, along with their able-bodied brothers and sisters. The focus is on the children—how they interact, and how they feel about each other. You will see what they look like. You can share these stories with your own children, who will enjoy learning about other young people who are successfully meeting challenges in their lives.

I met these families through caregivers, organizations, and activity centers for disabled children. I visited with each family on at least two separate occasions, photographing and taping conversations with the children and the adults. Everyone I approached agreed to participate and no one made privacy an issue. They were eager to tell their stories. All were proud of their children's progress, especially since the children have generally gone far beyond what had been expected or predicted.

Without a doubt, life in a household with special needs children is complicated and stressful. The "normal" routine of the family is turned upside down. However, these great challenges bring great rewards, as many families have discovered. This book is about the problems faced and lessons learned, about love and respect and responsibility among brothers and sisters. Most importantly, it is about compassion, acceptance, and the faith that great obstacles can be overcome through patience and dedication.

EVA

Eva is twelve. She has stepsisters Elana, fifteen, and Elysa, five.

Down's syndrome has slowed Eva's physical and mental development, but it hasn't limited her energy. She is in a special education class in school, but takes mainstream classes for different subjects at different grade levels, depending on her abilities. For example, she goes to gym class with the fifth grade, reading with the third grade, and arithmetic with the second grade. She also attends an after-school and summer program at a community center for developmentally disabled children, as well as an art institute for people with disabilities. She loves art and music. At home, when she has time to herself, her favorite activity is dancing to music on her stereo.

According to her sister Elana, Eva shows her artistic flair by dressing in her own unique style, choosing unusual, flamboyant color combinations. "Another thing about Eva," Elana discloses, "is she likes to eat ketchup on all her food—macaroni and cheese, toast, eggs, anything! It's kind of gross."

At her mother's house, Eva plays games with five-year-old Elysa, and they get along well. On alternate weekends, when Eva visits her father, she plays with his friend's nine-year-old daughter, Amber. But Amber is growing up at a faster pace than Eva, and the two girls are less compatible than they used to be. Eva is growing up, too, becoming a teenager, but her development is inconsistent. Elana describes what is happening: "She's pretty much a teenage girl; it's just that some things are different. Like, she'll still watch *Sesame Street*. In some areas she's really brilliant, but in some areas she's held back."

Elana talks about what it is like to have a sister with a disability. "I used to wish that Eva was 'normal' so I could talk about more stuff with her and feel I could communicate with her, because my next sister [Elysa] is five years old and I can't talk to her. Eva looks up to me a lot. She'll copy me. It used to be annoying when I was twelve or thirteen. But now I think it's kind of flattering that she wants to be like me," she admits. When she was little, Elana wasn't aware that Eva was different, "she was such a cute baby." Gradually, she realized that it was taking Eva "longer to learn how to walk and go to the bathroom and stuff. When I was about eight or nine, I started getting a little bit embarrassed about her." Even now, "I still have a little problem, but she's my sister and I can't pretend that she's not there."

Elana reflects on what is wonderful and special about having Eva for a sister. "If I'm upset or something, I can go into Eva's room and she's there for me. She won't pass judgment on anybody. And she's never going to say anything bad about somebody unless they've done something bad to her. And that's nice." By comparison, "a normal teenage girl is going to be superficial. Eva has made me more compassionate toward people with disabilities or learning problems. Even with my friends I'm not so quick to pass judgment, because you never know what's going on in someone's family." There is pride in her voice when she talks about herself and Eva. "She's taught me a lot, she's pissed me off a lot—but she's Eva."

KURT

Kurt is four. His brother Karl is nine.

Kurt's mother recalls that they used to call him "the baby from hell." At age two, he was exceptionally strong and well-coordinated. He was also clever, stubborn, and wild, which probably helped him survive severe head injuries from a motorcycle accident. His toughness, an intensive rehabilitation program, and a special big brother are helping him regain his physical skills and catch up with where he should be at his age. His brother Karl, who is five years older, is kind, gentle, loving, and extraordinarily well-adjusted. Everyone agrees that he is Kurt's most effective therapist. Their mother comments wryly that if their roles were reversed and Karl had been the one injured, "he would be in serious trouble."

Kurt was riding behind his dad on a three-wheel motorbike when they hit something in the road. The bike flipped over and Kurt was thrown. At first he was not expected to live. He was in a coma for six weeks. When he came out of the coma, he was unable to move or even swallow. He still couldn't walk or sit up when he came home after four months in the hospital. Now, nearly two years later, he can run, catch a ball, and ride a bike, even though he is still a bit uncoordinated. His cognitive development and communication skills are weak, but he tries very hard and is improving steadily.

His brother Karl has had a lot to do with Kurt's progress. Karl almost never seems to run out of patience. He urges Kurt to talk, makes him repeat words until he pronounces them correctly, and encourages him to say complete sentences. Karl gives an example: "When he says, 'I cream,' I say, 'What about ice cream?' Then he says, 'I want ice cream.' And I say, 'What's the magic word?' He says, 'Please.'" Karl also plays learning games on the computer with him and occasionally lets him play Nintendo, although Kurt just randomly presses buttons. Outside, the boys play ball games. Karl explains how he lets Kurt have the advantage now and then, giving him a chance to win. Karl admits that he sometimes is annoyed with his little brother, particularly when he has his own friends over from school. He explains, "Kurt has fun when we're playing outside, but sometimes he doesn't want to come in with us, and we can't leave him out by himself."

Kurt participates in an early intervention program through the public school and is in a class for communicatively handicapped children. His parents are delighted with the progress he has made, but they realize that he probably won't be able to go to school with Karl. (His school is not equipped for children with special needs.)

Kurt will soon start playing ball in a league for kids with disabilities, and Karl will cheer him on. "While we want Karl to spend time with Kurt, we want him to have a life of his own, too," their parents say. They take Karl on special trips and make sure he gets his fair share of attention.

Considering how badly he was injured, Kurt has made an amazing recovery. His mother says, "I think love brought Kurt through." His survival might also have something to do with the fact that he has always been a tough little guy—and his big brother Karl has always been a "real good kid."

ALOPA

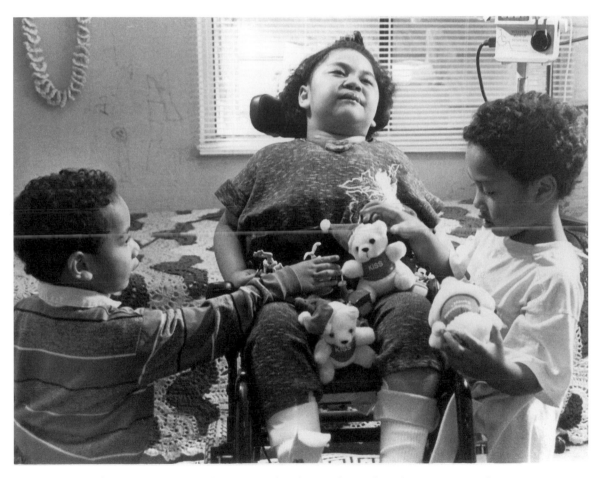

Alopa is almost six. She has four brothers: Christopher, four; Spencer, three;
Nuku, two; and Fotu Junior, eight months.

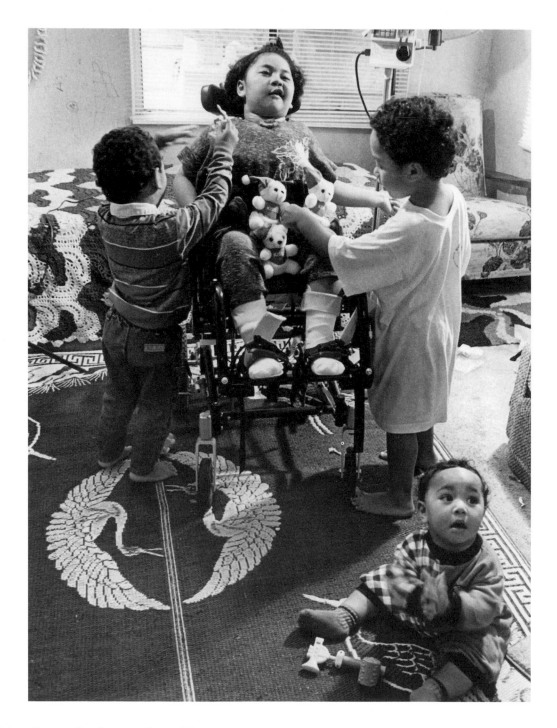

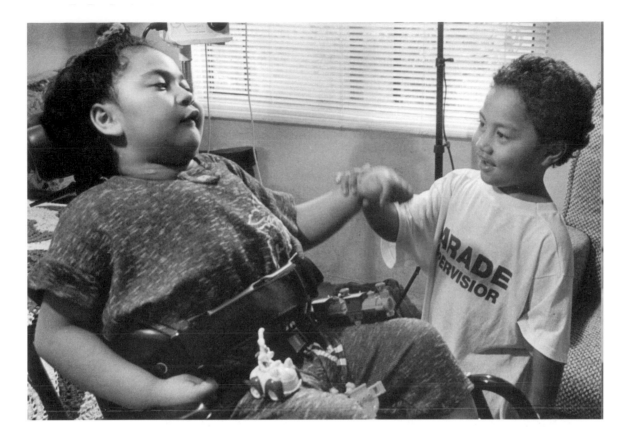

Three of Alopa's little brothers saw her run into the street just as the car raced down the hill. The young men in the car were high on drugs. The driver tried to avoid hitting her, but couldn't control the car. Alopa sustained brain and spinal cord damage, and several broken bones. She was in a coma for more than a month. Nuku was too young to be aware of the accident, but Christopher and Spencer, who were older, had nightmares for months afterward. They still sometimes scream in panic when they hear sirens, afraid that Alopa will be taken away again. Ten months later, she is home, and the boys are beginning to feel that the family is safe again.

Alopa can't talk; she is paralyzed and has to be fed through a tube in her stomach, but she is improving. Her mother has noticed that "she moves her eyes and turns her head a little bit when people around her are talking or laughing." She is also beginning to regain some movement in her hands and legs. And she smiles a lot.

Their parents say that "her brothers are right there to make her smile. They move her hands, put toys on her lap, and dance and sing for her." After school and on weekends, her cousins come to the house to play with her. Even though she can't speak, she manages to show how happy she is to have them around.

Alopa needs a great deal of care—washing and diapering, frequent transfers between bed and wheelchair, and five tube feedings a day. Christopher and Spencer help by entertaining her, when they're not watching *Sesame Street* or other children's television programs. "The boys aren't old enough to go to regular school and we worry about what might happen when we aren't watching them," their parents say. They are concerned about the dangerous streets in their inner-city neighborhood—streets with potholes, poor visibility, and not enough stop signs—and about careless drivers.

Life is difficult for the family these days, but they are grateful for the care Alopa received at Children's Hospital and the progress she has made in the ten months since the accident. The man who caused the accident has been apprehended and punished, but Alopa's parents are less concerned with retribution than with drugs and unsafe streets. As for Alopa, she responds a little more everyday to their hugs, their singing, and their prayers. They are holding on to their faith that she will get better, that one day she will walk and talk again with her brothers.

HOANG AND MICHAEL

Hoang is fourteen and Michael is six. Their sister Elizabeth is seventeen, and their brothers Peter and Carter are ten and fifteen.

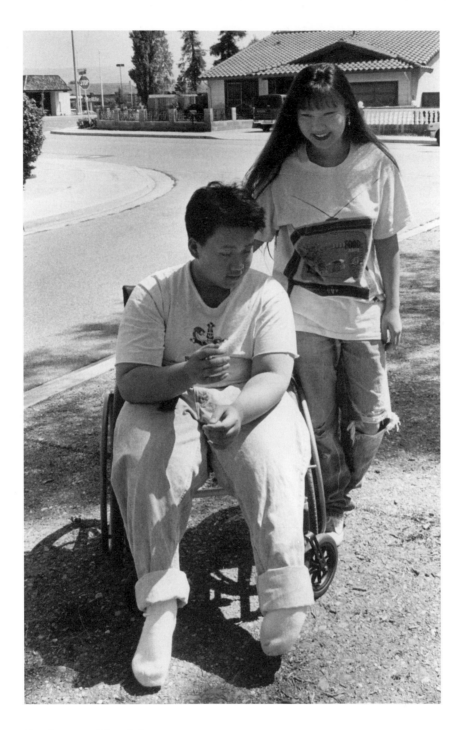

Sisters, Brothers, and Disability

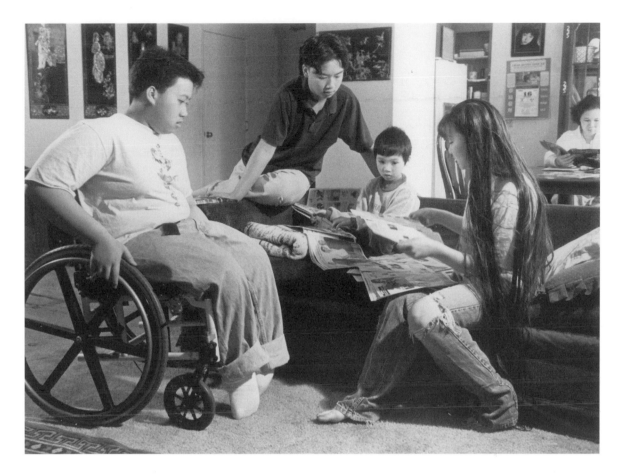

oang's mother is convinced that her childhood exposure to Agent Orange caused her son's spina bifida. He has other medical complications as well—infections, skin rashes, digestive problems, fevers, and terrible headaches—but he is improving, and the bad times don't come as often as they once did. Hoang's youngest brother Michael is also handicapped—he was born with a heart defect that required surgery when he was a baby. Today, Michael is still limited in his physical activities.

The children's mother came to the United States from Vietnam in 1976. She met and married her husband in the United States, and all the children were born here. Although the other three children seem to have escaped health deficiencies, it is hard for their parents to see Michael and Hoang suffer. Their mother feels responsible. Her

English is awkward, but she speaks eloquently when she describes what she has seen and experienced. She describes her hometown. "I see a lot of people born, children, no hand, no leg. I see some kid born, normal but no eyeball. And I see disease of the skin, there is no treatment. And I say, 'What caused these problems?' But I cannot get the answer."

Their parents place great value on the family, and try to keep their children close to home.

Peter, Carter, and Elizabeth help care for Hoang and Michael, but Hoang doesn't need help anymore. "I can take care of myself, most of the time," he says with pride. But there are tensions, too. Hoang admits that he and Carter "get in fights a lot and Elizabeth tries to make us make up." Hoang has many friends "who help me out," he says. When he has questions or personal problems, he talks to his doctor or the nurse at Children's Hospital who has cared for him since he was a child.

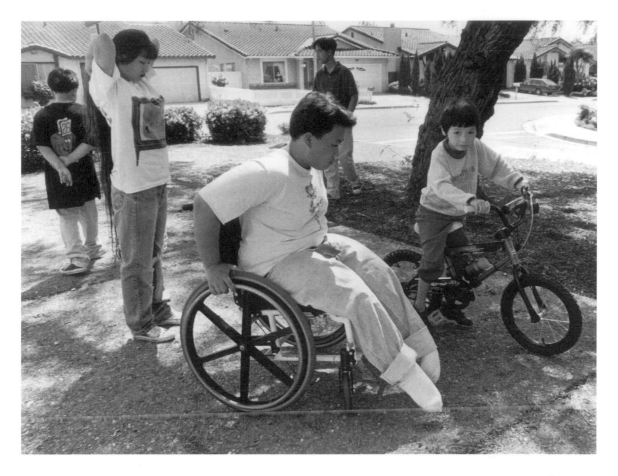

All the children seem to have a talent for drawing, but Peter has been the most successful. Hoang declares with pride that his brother has just been accepted for a special summer art program for promising young artists.

Everyone in this family is motivated to be successful, and Hoang is no exception. "I'll be disabled for life," he says. "That's what the doctor told me. But that won't stop me from doing whatever I want to do."

GREGORY AND KRISTA

Gregory is six and a half. Krista is six. Their brother Calvin is two.

Gregory and Krista both have spina bifida and hydrocephalus. They live with their parents (Greg's mother and Krista's father married three years ago) and two-year-old Calvin, the little brother they both adore. The first years of their lives were vastly different, and these differences are reflected in their personalities.

Greg and his mother lived in the San Francisco Bay area, where people with disabilities have long been visible and active in the community. Disabled children are integrated in play groups, neighborhoods, and schools, and their parents have access to support groups and services. Krista, on the other hand, spent her first years in rural Florida, cared for by her father and grandmother. Most of the time she sat passively in the company of adults. There were no preschool programs; she had few playmates. Furthermore, the attitude toward disability in the area can best be described as medieval. Parents are pitied, the child is seen as a burden, and the "best" thing to be hoped for is that "The good Lord will take the child soon."

Greg's mother and Krista's father met at a spina bifida association's national conference in Texas three years ago, and it didn't take them long to fall in love. Attractive, energetic single parents, they immediately formed a strong bond. Greg's mother reminisces: "We both understood bowel management. We understood cathing. We understood you can't just pick up and go, everything has to be planned. We understood stress from surgeries. We understood the dream that was gone. We talked about that and understood how it feels to lose a dream, then go from there and make a whole new dream for yourself and your child. And we decided a week later to get married."

They settled in Florida, in a rural area that would provide a safe, peaceful environment for the new family. Within the year, Calvin was born—a healthy, boisterous boy who would be outrageously spoiled and doted on by his sister and brother. Like their parents, Greg and Krista bonded immediately, and Krista especially thrived under the exuberant love of her new brother. She threw off her passivity and became more verbal and assertive. She began to make friends. Krista showed unbounded admiration of Greg, and delighted in the antics of little Calvin. Greg, who has a cheerful, outgoing personality and is accustomed to being accepted by everyone, immediately made new friends. He was "adopted" by the local fire department. They gave him pictures, badges, and a special set of fireman's clothes. It was a grand time for Greg, and he decided to be a fireman when he grows up. "If not an actual firefighter," his mother suggests, "he could be a dispatcher in a fire station."

Living in the country, however, turned out to be too difficult. The many services the children needed—doctors, therapists, and community programs—required traveling great distances or were not available at all. So last year, the family moved to the San Francisco Bay area. Greg started kindergarten and Krista is enrolled in special education. Both children have had numerous medical problems and frequent surgeries related to their spina bifida and hydrocephalus. Krista has had additional problems with infections and cysts forming in her brain that might cause future complications.

Recently, a broken blood vessel in Krista's brain left her paralyzed from the neck down. Despite her difficulties, she apparently has only a slight learning disability and is one of the top students in her class. She is even learning to use a computer. She talks and communicates well, and she is popular with her schoolmates. Krista loves going to school and happily reels off a list of all her friends. At home she laughs gleefully, egging Calvin on as he climbs all over Greg, causing Greg to yelp and shout when things get a bit too rough for him.

Their parents are preparing the children to lead lives as full and independent as possible. Their mother says, "Medical needs are very important, and we are making sure the children realize how important it is to take care of their bodies." Their father adds, "education is a top priority, too. We know that our kids will go to college." They would like Krista to be a writer, their mother says. Krista agrees, declaring, "I'll write songs, Greg will play the guitar, and Calvin will sing."

With two disabled children, an energetic two-year-old, and two very boisterous dogs, there is a lot of stress in this family. But the love and appreciation the kids and parents have for each other is expressed openly and frequently. They emphasize what they can do, instead of what they can't. What counts is that Krista can talk and taste and love and laugh. Greg can sing and shout and move his arms about. Does it bother him that he can't walk? He responds with a six-year-old's bravado, "Forget it!"

PORTIA

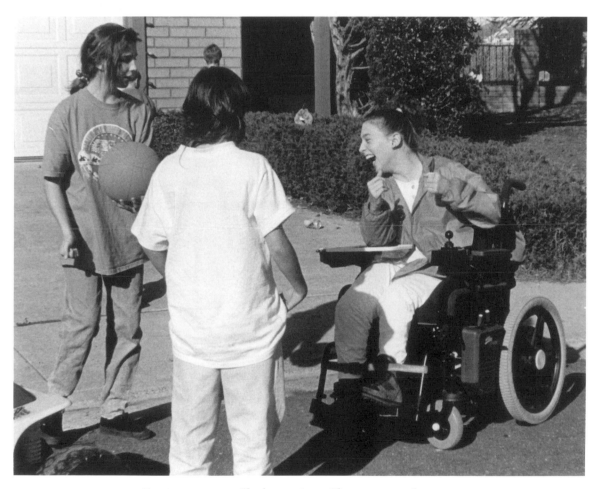

Portia is sixteen. She has a sister, Shannon, age thirteen,
and two brothers: Frankie, twelve, and Casey, four.

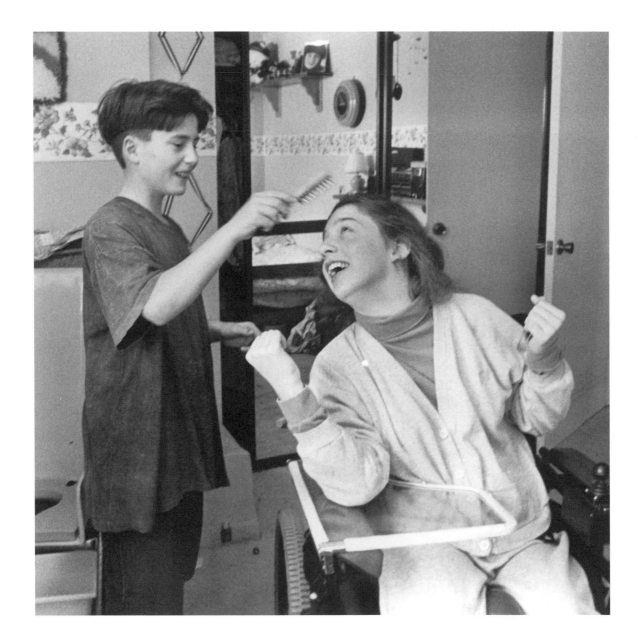

Portia says she doesn't often play outside. She has to spend a lot of time on her schoolwork. "I don't write very fast because of cerebral palsy," she explains. She's taking all the required tenth grade classes at school, as well as an elective in which she works with a disabled third grader. Portia declares firmly, "When I graduate from high school, I will move out and go to college. Probably I'll go back to Berkeley." Eventually she expects to "work with disabled kids and computers."

A little over a year ago, Portia and her family moved to a small town thirty miles from Berkeley. Like most teenagers who move to a new neighborhood, Portia is finding it hard to adjust. She misses her friends and all the activities available in Berkeley. And there are few disabled people in her new town. Portia tells about a girl she met named Lisa, who is severely disabled. "Every time I went into Raley's to go shopping, they would say, 'Hi, Lisa.' I would turn around and say, 'I'm not Lisa.'" Explaining that people don't often look at her face, she comments bitterly, "they think every female who comes into their store in a wheelchair is Lisa!"

Shannon is three years younger and very different from Portia. She loves sports and spends most of her time playing outdoors. Shannon says, "Sometimes I'll paint Portia's nails or do stuff like that," but it is clear that most of the time she would rather be shooting baskets outside.

Portia likes to go to Berkeley to visit her friends, but so far, she hasn't worked up enough confidence to make the train trip by herself. When she goes, Frankie comes along. He is only twelve, but his parents trust him to help his sister. To Portia, Frankie is the special person in the family, and he admits, "Portia is my all-time favorite person." Frankie is the one most sensitive to her needs, and Portia says, "I can talk to him about anything that's on my mind." On the other hand, he can be the typical twelve-year-old little brother who is not above complaining. And he expresses just a tiny bit of envy over the long ride Portia got in the sidecar on their dad's motorcycle last month. Portia says, "I loved it!" Frankie liked the sidecar, too, "but I only got to ride around the block."

Shannon and Frankie take turns helping Portia get ready every morning, putting on her clothes, leg braces, and shoes, and combing her hair. "It's one of their household chores, and if they don't feel like doing it, they have to do it anyway," Portia declares smugly. Shannon admits that "it's more fun than making sandwiches." Little Casey helps sometimes, taking off her shoes and braces if Portia asks him. Portia has chores, too. Shannon says that "Portia does her homework and helps out when we have company." Portia also helps at an agency where parents, teachers, and people with disabilities work together to connect disabled youngsters with appropriate technologies. Her mother works there as a resource specialist, and Portia often goes in with her on days when there is no school.

Portia is approaching a difficult age for teenagers, alternating between wanting to grow up and wanting the protection of her parents. She is keenly aware of her restrictions and knows that her disability makes her different from other people her age. Sometimes she gets depressed, but she is a strong person, reflecting the support of a warm and loving family. "I am going to be independent and I know what I want to do with my life," Portia says. There is no doubt that she will succeed.

JENNIFER

Jennifer is twelve. Her sister Caitlin is six.

Until three years ago, Jennifer was an avid soccer player and the youngest member of a team that traveled all over northern California. But while hiking in the mountains with her day camp group, she had a fall that broke two vertebrae and crushed her spinal cord, leaving her a paraplegic. Soccer had been the center of her life, she reflects. "I was very upset about losing that, and it took a while to get used to it. But about five or six months later, I was used to it." She began participating in wheelchair sports and now competes in track and field, plays basketball, and plays tennis whenever she can find a partner.

During the three months that Jennifer was in the hospital, the entire family rallied to help. Relatives traveled from the east coast to look after Caitlin, who was three years old at the time, while her parents spent time with Jennifer. When Jennifer came home, she had relearn how to take care of herself. Their parents say, "We all had a lot of adjustments to make." The entire family learned to accept each others' limitations as well as their own, to ask for and give help, and to consider each others' feelings. Caitlin says she wasn't jealous of the attention that Jennifer got, just of all the stuffed animals. Jennifer laughs. "Yeah, I got about fourteen thousand stuffed animals." Caitlin adds, "But then she gave them to me." Her eyes light up as she remembers a panda bear she especially liked.

The accident happened the summer before Jennifer entered fourth grade. She went back to school with her old friends, but they seemed

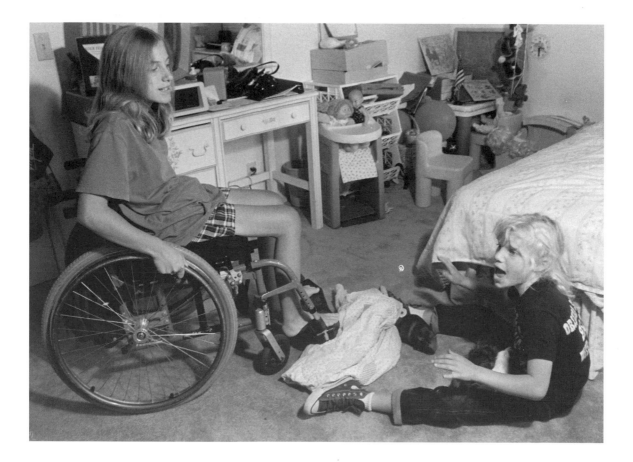

to drift away. She describes the experience without anger. "They dumped me," she says. "I don't know if it was because they didn't like me or because I was in a chair." She soon became involved with a new group of young people. When she started junior high last year, she made a lot of new friends. "People say I'm popular," she says matter-of-factly.

Jennifer has a positive outlook and has put her unpleasant experiences behind her. But her mother remembers that there were some bad times. She recalls the day when Jennifer came home in tears. "Some of her classmates had gone to the teacher behind her back to complain that she was being pushy and making too many demands for help." Her mother confronted the teacher, encouraging her to bring the situation out into the open. She pointed out that Jennifer only wanted to be treated like everyone else. If the children felt uncomfortable talking in front of Jennifer, certainly Jennifer felt uncomfortable knowing they were talking behind her back. In the end, everyone learned from the experience.

Jennifer manages all her own personal care and is quite independent. She is also responsible for babysitting Caitlin when their parents go out. Caitlin describes herself as "a helpful kid." Jennifer really doesn't need much help, but if Caitlin holds her wheelchair, it is much easier for Jennifer to transfer into it and she appreciates that assistance. Caitlin doesn't have to be asked. She seems intuitively sensitive to other people's needs. She explains, "If I see someone having trouble with something, I don't have to think about it, I just help them."

The girls' father has always been an enthusiastic volunteer, helping with school and sports activities. Now he has added Jennifer's wheelchair sports program to his many interests. Their mother has returned to her management job, which she had given up temporarily to care for Jennifer. She admits that she likes to have a clean, orderly house, but that is pretty hard to manage these days. She says ruefully, "I had to get used to having my walls all banged up by wheelchairs. There's no corner in this house that hasn't been touched by wheels."

Jennifer enjoys her popularity in school and her successes at sports. But she is happiest, she says, when she is involved in an activity with a friend and the friend "completely forgets that I'm in a wheelchair."

ROCIO

Rocio is seventeen. Her sister Andrea is ten.

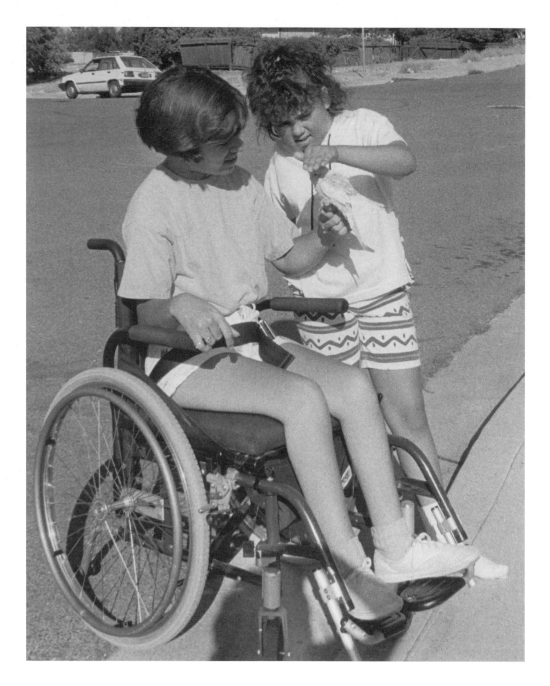

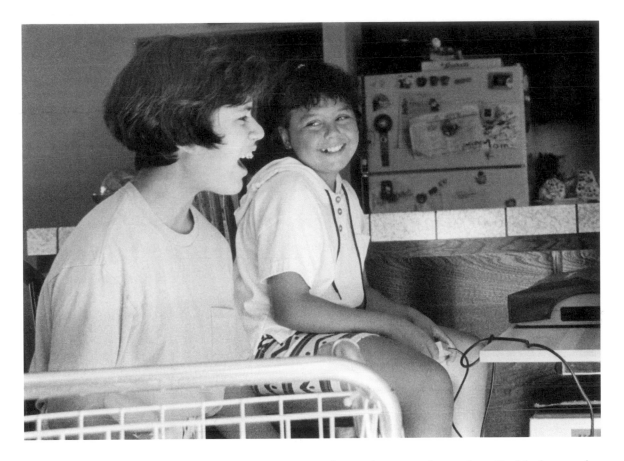

At seventeen, Rocio is almost grown up. She is making plans for college and her parents are buying and outfitting a van for her to drive. It will be a big help to the family when she can chauffeur her little sister Andrea to school and dance lessons, and it will give Rocio some freedom and independence. Rocio has cerebral palsy and uses a wheelchair, but she is able to transfer in and out of it and often uses a walker at home. The family lives in a small town with few, if any, obviously disabled people. Consequently, she sometimes has problems with poor access and public insensitivity. Rocio has often had to wait an hour or more to get home from school because a bus with a lift is either unavailable or broken down. She had a teacher who scolded her for always coming late to her Spanish class, which happened to be right after lunch. Rocio explained, "There wasn't enough time to eat lunch and go to the bathroom, because the only restroom I could

MARK

Mark is almost twelve. His sister Karen is thirteen.

When Karen was four years old and she and Mark were playing in the park, a little boy started teasing Mark because he was in a wheelchair. Karen scolded the boy: "Your mother didn't do a very good job raising you, because if she had you'd know it's not polite to make fun of kids in wheelchairs." She is thirteen now and Mark is almost twelve, and she still has to deal with people who patronize Mark for his disability or stigmatize her because she is the sibling of a disabled child.

Mark was born with spina bifida. As his father describes his initial reactions to Mark's disability and the realization that this was a child "who is not going to be in Little League, a child who is not going to run around and ride bicycles—all the normal things." Karen interrupts: "What makes normal? I don't know what it would be like to have a brother who isn't in a wheelchair, so to me it's normal." She doesn't remember life without Mark.

For their parents, having Mark brought about a change in their lifestyle and values. Mark's father talks about our society's preoccupation with the concept of perfection, whether it be the perfect house, the perfect car, or the perfect body. "All that goes away when you have a handicapped child, because there's just no chance for it. It becomes a non-value."

The parents explain, "What is important is how you get your family and your child integrated into a society that is accepting and nurturing." They have found allies among other families with disabled children, and they relish the diversity of this community. Their children also enjoy a broad range of friendships.

However, they live in a conservative suburban area where Mark is the only disabled student in the school, so both Mark and Karen encounter ignorance and insensitivity. When Karen's teachers find out about Mark, they tend to label her the "sister of a disabled child," which somehow makes her different from the other youngsters. But Karen is learning to be assertive, to demand that she be treated like everyone else. Yes, she is Mark's sister, but the fact that he is disabled is irrelevant. For Mark, the struggle is not so much against the stigma attached to disabled people, but for his right to equal educational opportunity. In spite of state and federal mandates, school officials balk at spending money on special needs, even something as basic as wheelchair-accessible bathrooms.

Many of the family activities center around Mark's involvement in sports. He competes in basketball, track and field, and the wheelchair equivalent of cross-country racing, all of which require regular practice and travel to out-of-town events. He also participates in the annual 7.5-mile San Francisco Bay to Breakers race, where his team of wheelchair riders tie themselves together to form a caterpillar and use their combined strength to get over the steep hills.

Because they are so close in age, Karen and Mark are pretty equal in their household responsibilities, and there are things they do to help each other. "I'll get him a glass of water if he'll do my laundry," Karen says with a laugh. Outside, Mark might get out of his wheelchair and roll around on the ground with his dog, while Karen settles herself in his chair. Sometimes she rolls off in it, which makes him angry, but she never makes him too angry. If they encounter a spot that's hard for him to negotiate in his chair, she pushes him without being asked.

Mom, Dad, Karen, Mark, and their dog Shadow may not fit the description of the average, traditional family, but they show that any family can be "normal."

AMY

Amy is eleven. Her sister Gina is eight; brother Kevin is four.

Amy was a long-awaited child, her mother reminisces. "It took ten years to conceive her." Then, when she was fifteen months old, a strange virus invaded her body, which resulted in a combination of devastating conditions that she was not expected to survive. Nobody knew what caused her condition or what could be done about it. Her parents recall feeling desperate and angry, but they also recall the many friends who gave them support and guidance. Amy's pediatrician was especially helpful and encouraging. Amy began therapy as soon as her condition was stable, and the program has helped her develop far beyond what was predicted for her at the time. Today, she is described as having "mild neuromuscular problems." She is in a special education program in a mainstream classroom, she moves unassisted with only minimal evidence of poor coordination, and she can express herself and relate to family and friends.

Gina was adopted when Amy was three and a half, and she turned out to be "a great blessing." Her mother explains that "if you have one child, and that child is disabled, you see that child's development as normal. I didn't really see Amy's differences until Gina came along." Furthermore, "Gina helped Amy pass through a lot of developmental stages"—not intentionally, it just happened. Amy would often copy Gina's behavior; because Gina could do something, Amy would try to do it, too. Their mother uses the word "modeling" to describe the process.

Developing language skills was a slow process for Amy, so the whole family learned sign language to help communicate with her. Their mother recalls how Gina, when she was nine months old, said her first word, "Dada," and signed "please" on the same day.

Gina is an active child who loves horseback riding. She often plays ball or other outdoor games with Amy. Kevin, adopted when he was six months old, has his own special relationship with Amy. They play with toys or look at picture books and pretend to read to each other. He still does not seem to be aware that she is disabled.

The children's grandmother, who has an advanced case of Alzheimer's, also lives with the family. Amy and Gina both like to help care for her, and all three youngsters are encouraged to "hang around" with their grandmother.

Gina now has conflicting feelings about having a disabled sister, and she is quite articulate in expressing herself. There are times when she resents Amy and complains that her sister is getting all the attention, but she will be "fiercely loyal to Amy in front of anybody who makes fun of her when they're out in public." Her mother has noticed, however, that "Gina will always introduce Amy as 'this is my handicapped sister Amy,' instead of 'this is my sister Amy, who just happens to have a handicap.'" Gina participates in a siblings' group organized by the parents' support group. This "gives her a place to vent her anger, her frustration, and her fears." She has friends in the group and enjoys going to the meetings.

Whatever anger and resentment Gina may feel, she delights in being a caretaker to Amy. "I bring her books and clean her room a lot, and I help her get down the stairs, and some-times I help her write. I help change her diaper, and help her get in bed, and I put the blankets on her."

One day Gina announced, "God made a mistake." Gina's parents were ready to respond with "God doesn't make mistakes," her mother says, "but we could see she'd been thinking about this, so we asked her what she meant. Gina explained, 'God knew Amy was going to be handicapped, so he should have let me be born first so that I could take care of her.'"

EMILE AND LAMILE

Emile and his twin brother Lamile are nine. Their brother Juwan is eleven.

Everyone in town who is involved with children, sports, or people with disabilities knows the Perry twins. Emile especially attracts attention with his bright smile as he zips around at top speed in his power wheelchair. The twins were born prematurely and both have cerebral palsy, but Emile is more severely disabled than Lamile. Emile was hydrocephalic and still has an internal shunt to drain fluid from his brain into his stomach. Lamile had difficulty breathing and was on a breathing machine. They were tiny when they were born, "about the size of teddy bears," their mother recalls.

The boys, second-graders in a regular public school, are rarely apart. They attend therapy sessions and take swimming lessons together, play wheelchair basketball, and spend their summers at local recreation centers. Their ninth birthday is coming up, and they're planning to celebrate with their many friends and relatives.

Emile has been using a power wheelchair for three years—he operates it like a race car. Lamile, who has difficulty walking, uses a chair when he participates in the wheelchair sports program with his brother. He already has had one operation to straighten his legs, and the doctors are proposing more surgery.

The boys' eleven-year-old brother Juwan has a learning disability and a speech problem, which apparently resulted from severe seizures he had when he was very young. He is in the fifth grade at a special school. Like his brothers, he enjoys sports and loves to talk about football and baseball. The boys' mother also takes care of two-year-old Miko, who stays with them every day. Miko has become almost part of the family, and she manages to hold her own when playing with the boys.

Emile and Lamile are both good students. Lamile states, "I really like going to the library," and Emile immediately says that he does, too. In addition to his regular schoolwork, Emile uses learning programs on a computer at home and at school.

Their mother has strong opinions about parents who keep their disabled children out of sight or put them in institutions. She is proud of Emile and doesn't hesitate to take him with her wherever she goes. "People are always talking to him, but sometimes kids will tease him or call him names." There are times when Emile feels low, when he wishes he could get up and walk and do the things that other people can do. His mother tells him, "other children may be blessed because they can walk, but you are blessed because you can ride in a wheelchair." Emile is most unhappy when his electric wheelchair is down for repairs. He cannot manipulate a manual chair, and it can be very dispiriting for this active youngster to be stuck in the house without his "wheels."

The boys' mother feels sorry for disabled kids who are neglected, and she plans to take in foster children when her own youngsters no longer need so much attention. She is sure that Juwan, Emile, and Lamile will lead productive, independent lives and that all the boys will continue to give love and joy to her and everyone they meet.

SEAN

Sean is four. His sister Tara is seven.

Sean, Tara, and their parents live on Shawn Drive in a neighborhood called Tara Hills. That's not quite coincidental, their mother says. She's Irish, and they chose the area because of its Irish heritage and Irish names. The children have quiet streets and lots of space where they can play.

Sean was diagnosed with Down's syndrome shortly after he was born. After the initial shock wore off, his parents joined a support group and soon became active in the Down's Syndrome League. They speak matter-of-factly about his disability. "Because of his special needs, we simply have to spend more time with him than we would with an average child." They take advantage of every opportunity to teach him as much as possible. His development is slower than average, but that doesn't seem to dampen his interest in learning.

Although he's three years old, Sean is just now entering his "terrible twos," which began, his mother recalls, when he tried to climb in the oven when it was turned on. He learned the word "hot" on that day, his father jokes. His parents' calm acceptance of Sean is reflected in Tara's attitude toward her little brother. If someone asks, she will say that her brother is handicapped; but the issue rarely seems to come up. When they play together, Tara is quiet and gentle, while Sean is generally noisy and exuberant.

"Sean doesn't talk much—he only knows about twenty or thirty words—but he does a lot of babbling," his mother says. She is not sure if he's making up words or actually trying to say something. His father is sure that "Sean knows what he means even if other people don't understand him." In school, Sean is learning sign language as part of a process called total communication. Signing seems to be easier for him than speaking, and he understands more when he can see and hear a word at the same time. Sean's parents and Tara are also learning to sign. Tara demonstrates: "Yellow bird, yellow bird fly away. Come back another day," she recites as she signs.

There is a lot of activity and laughter in this household, and both children get plenty of attention. Their parents hope that Tara will always "be there emotionally for her brother without feeling that he is a burden." It looks like their parent's hopes will be fulfilled. Tara and Sean are happy, loving youngsters and will surely be the same when they are grown up.

EFREN

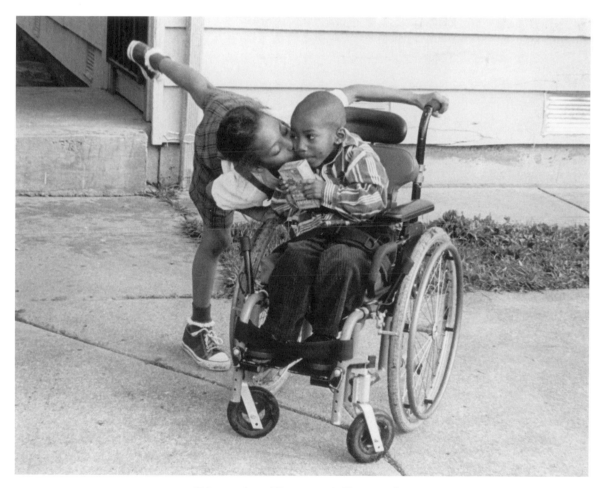

Efren is four. His sister Ashley is eight.

On a March day not quite two years ago, Efren and his father were sitting in the car about to go visit his grandmother. Efren was a bright two-year-old—walking, talking, already potty-trained. His father was an outgoing, fast-moving man—a man who had enemies. "They walked up to the car and they shot him in the head, and then they shot my son. His father died instantly. Efren was in the hospital for almost a year and a half." She reflects, "You always know who you don't like, but you never know who doesn't like you. Why did they shoot little Efren? That's how life goes in the ghetto. Stuff like that happens every day in the neighborhood. It's not a surprise to see—but it hurts when it's yours."

The bullet entered Efren's face, angled down through his neck and ribs, and came out his back. He was paralyzed from the neck down, although with the treatments he had in the hospital and with continuing therapy, he has regained the use of his arms. He continues to improve. His mother, devastated by the loss of the man she loved, struggled to help Efren and his sister Ashley understand what had happened. Ashley had just turned seven at the time of the shooting, and she had no idea what it meant to die, to be shot, or to be paralyzed. "It helped to go to her father's funeral," her mother says, "and to spend time with her brother in the hospital."

Efren doesn't remember much of what happened, but he remembers that he used to be able to walk. He sometimes gets frustrated at not being able to run and play with other children. "But that only makes his determination

stronger," his mother says. "He manages to move that wheelchair wherever he wants to go." Efren had nightmares at first, and was given medication to stop them. His bad dreams trouble him less frequently now. He misses his father and often pretends that he is there with him. He tells his mother, "My daddy told me to tell you 'hi,'" to which she responds, "Tell him I said 'hi.'" She has told him that his daddy is asleep—that he will sleep for a long time, but Efren will see him again in heaven. Recently she took him to the cemetery. He brought along a little picture he had made at school and put it on his father's grave.

Efren is surrounded by a large and supportive extended family. During the first six months after the shooting, when Efren's condition remained critical, relatives came from all over the country to help out. "I talked and read to him while he was still in the hospital," Ashley says. She still helps care for him and even gives him his baths. She plays with Efren, too, and sometimes picks on him and teases him. Like any eight-year-old girl with an energetic little brother, she sometimes gets tired of him and runs off to play with her girlfriends. She is a smart little girl who enjoys dancing and gymnastics—Efren and his mother call her "Flipper," with good reason.

The children have had to learn to be wary of strangers, but "in the neighborhood all the cousins look after each other," their mother says. Efren has plenty of playmates among his numerous cousins and friends at school. He is an exceptionally bright and sociable young-ster—his mother comments that he is "bossy"—and she is sure that nobody treats him differently because he is handicapped.

Efren's favorite cousin and best friend is eleven-year-old Dion, the only other boy in the immediate family. He lives in another part of town, but he is at Efren's house almost every day. He plays with Efren and takes him for walks. Not long ago, Dion saved up his allowance to buy a two-piece necklace that said "Best Friends." He gave one piece to Efren and kept the other for himself.

Efren still needs a great deal of attention. He and his wheelchair have to be carried up and down the stairs to and from their apartment—Dion and some of the older children often help. He has to be catheterized every three hours—only his mother will do that. Efren also attends regular therapy sessions. Their mother is getting her life in order and gaining confidence in her own ability to cope. She is determined to teach the children how to sur-vive, deal with their fears, and grow up strong—sure that they can handle whatever life holds for them. This family has come a long way in the last two years.

TALIA

Talia is seven. Her sister Sara is three.

Talia used to go to preschool with a number of other children with disabilities, but she transferred to a public school when she entered first grade last year. She can maneuver herself quite well in her new school, though she occasionally has to ask a friend or teacher for a push. Her school has only one other child who uses a wheelchair, which, unlike Talia's, is a power chair. Talia is intrigued by it. "Loren pushes that black button and the lights blink which way she is going," she explains.

Sara goes to a private nursery school, but every once in a while their mother takes her to visit Talia's school. Talia loves it, and shows Sara off to all her friends. Sara likes it when Talia comes to her school, too. Recently, on a day when Talia's school was closed, she offered to go to school with Sara and read to the younger children. Talia was such a success with her little sister's classmates that the teacher invited her to come again. Both girls felt very proud.

Sara, like Talia, also has health problems. She was born prematurely, like her sister, and remained in the hospital for several months. She continued to require special attention after she came home. Their parents explain that a large part of the family's time is spent in sessions with therapists. "And doctors," Talia chimes in, "and nurses." "And eye drops," Sara adds.

At home the girls spend their time together, often engaged in different activities but in the same room. Their relationship is becoming more and more reciprocal, their parents say.

Sara can fetch, carry, and retrieve things that are out of Talia's reach. "Talia reads to Sara and teaches her the things she is learning in school," says their mother. "She tries to help wash Sara in the bathtub, and in the morning she helps Sara choose which clothes to wear and even tries to help dress her."

Talia is a role model for Sara. She also has a quick mind and a decided bent toward mischief, which will no doubt provide many challenges to their parents as she and Sara wend their way toward adulthood.

TICO

Tico is six. His sister Julie is two.

84   *Sisters, Brothers, and Disability*

Tico was almost three years old before he was diagnosed as autistic. Physically his development was normal, but he had unusual behavior patterns. "He wouldn't respond when people talked to him, although he obviously wasn't deaf, since he could hear the ice cream truck coming up the street," his parents say. "He often had tantrums, and was extremely upset by loud noises, like the vacuum cleaner or blender." He had to touch everything. Tico had a tendency to break things, and his movements were uncoordinated, so he was in constant danger of hurting himself. To find out what was wrong, he and his parents trudged from clinic to clinic and hospital to hospital. Tico was given batteries of tests to follow up each tentative diagnosis offered by physicians,

psychologists, therapists, and teachers. "They tested for lead," his father recalls. "They took blood tests, urine tests, hearing tests, psychological tests, all kinds of tests, until Tico was afraid to go near a hospital because he knew that something terrible would happen to him there." Through it all, his parents admit sadly, they were waiting for a definitive answer, "looking for somebody to tell us there was nothing wrong with him," but knowing all the time that this was an impossible hope.

"It was hard to accept his disability," his mother says. His father explains, "Physically he's normal, but mentally he's disabled—this is autism. It's not like being in a wheelchair, where you can see the disability. We can talk to him. Sometimes he responds, and sometimes he doesn't. He's there physically, but he's not there mentally."

Tico's parents are from Guatemala. They have lived in the United States for many years and have a support system of many relatives here. Socializing is limited because visiting anywhere with Tico is difficult. "We have to watch him all the time. He keeps touching stuff and going all over the place so we can't let him out of our sight."

Tico thrived under the guidance of a skilled and loving teacher in an early childhood special education program. "We were so lucky to have that teacher," his father declares. "She was a wonderful person. She helped us a lot, she touched our family. And she loved Tico." Therapy has also improved Tico's behavior and ability to communicate.

His little sister Julie was born when Tico was four. His parents say that his sister has changed Tico. "He has mellowed." When his mother was pregnant with Julie, his parents worried that Tico might hurt the new baby. Just before Julie was born, they became particularly anxious when a friend's son became so violent toward his baby sister that the boy had to be institutionalized. Tico's parents took great pains to prepare him. Their father says, "When Julie was born, I videotaped her in the hospital and showed Tico the video, and told him that this was his new baby sister." Tico came along when his mother and Julie came home from the hospital.

Tico bonded with Julie right away, although he had to be reminded to be gentle with her. Because he does not coordinate his movements very well, he could have unintentionally hurt her when she was a baby, but now she can hold her own with him. Julie and Tico interact in special ways. He sees that she is not frightened of the world the way he is, and he seems to gain courage from her. Their mother says, "He will try new foods, for example, if Julie will try them first." If he does not feel like playing with Julie, he has learned to respond gently. Sometimes he makes wild random motions, like jumping up and down and waving his arms around, and she will imitate him as if they were playing a game.

As the children grow, their relationship continues to change. Julie has entered her "terrible twos" and is getting a bit pushy. She will soon begin to realize that Tico is different from other children. Meanwhile, Tico, with the help of his therapists and teachers, is learning to communicate by pointing to pictures that he carries in his own special wallet. He needs his life to be very structured, and he gets upset when confronted with anything new or different. But he is learning to control his behavior and rarely has tantrums.

Before Tico was born, his parents knew nothing about autism. But now they have read every book they could find on the subject. Autism is still not understood, even by professionals in the field, and Tico's parents have had to figure out most things for themselves. They have tried a few of the many therapies and dietary regimens proposed by "experts." So far they have found that Tico's special education program has been the most effective tool in his development.

His parents agree that the most important thing they can give him "is love and a lot of patience." No one knows Tico's potential or what his life will be like, but with his parents to smooth the way and Julie to push him toward new experiences, his future looks promising.

RACHEL

Rachel is eleven. Her brother Nathan is seven.

Rachel is an easygoing child who dearly loves her Pooh Bear. She enjoys playing ball with her brother and a dozen friends whose names she can tick off in one breath. Her favorite activities at school, she declares, are lunch and recess. Rachel has poor motor coordination and difficulty processing language, manifestations of a syndrome the doctors still have not been able to identify. She began having seizures as an infant, but no one knows whether these were the cause of her brain damage, or the result.

Rachel's brother Nathan and his friends used to tease her because she behaved differently from them and was slow to learn physical and social skills. But Rachel is oblivious to teasing and when the boys realized they couldn't get a reaction out of her, the teasing soon stopped. Now that Nathan is older, he understands that making fun of Rachel is unacceptable behavior. He is learning to stand up to his friends and protect Rachel, and becoming more patient with her limitations as he matures.

Nathan attends a support group for siblings of special needs children. He doesn't talk much about what goes on in the group, but admits that "I learn a few things there and it's actually pretty nice." He wasn't so keen about it last week, he declares, because he didn't like the milk they served to the kids. His mother chides him, saying he should talk about the important things. Nathan insists, "Well, that's important." Nathan is still pretty focused on himself. When his parents ask him to explain what happens when Rachel has a seizure, he launches into a narration. "She has to go to the hospital, and we call somebody up late at night and ask them if I can spend the night there." He recalls the night when Rachel was sick and he went next door and got to stay up late to watch *Mary Poppins*. "For me it's fun," he says, but quickly adds, "For them it's not."

Rachel's difficulty in understanding and processing language seriously slowed her learning. Daily medication has helped bring Rachel's seizures under control, and she is improving her verbal and physical skills. She is in a special education program at their neighborhood school. Nathan has a scientific bent and attends an alternative school with a challenging curriculum. He is fascinated with minerals and can identify every piece in his enormous rock collection.

Nathan's presence has helped spur Rachel's development as well. When Nathan learned to talk, Rachel learned to speak as a way to imitate Nathan. Before she had a little brother, she was not interested in playing with other children, but preferred to sit quietly and listen to adults talking. Nathan taught Rachel how to play, and she plays both with him and her own friends. Their father says that "Rachel and Nathan play ball or chase soap bubbles together in the backyard," or engage in quiet games inside. They also share their own special "pretending" games.

Rachel's parents have exposed her to art and music, and though her fine motor coordination is not good enough for her to draw or play the piano successfully, she has a good sense of color and can sing very well. In fact, her mother says, "Rachel can carry a tune and was singing long before she could talk." Rachel is not adept at carrying on a conversation, but she is friendly and lovable, and people are drawn to her.

Even if Rachel were not disabled, these two children would be very different in their interests and personalities, but the fact that she has special needs is forging a unique bond between them.

OTIS

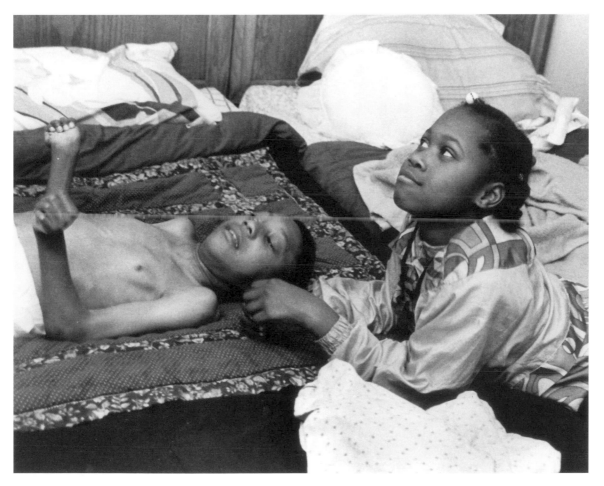

Otis is fifteen. His sister Quiana is nine.

"Otis is a real good fellow," his mother states. As a consequence of cerebral palsy, he can't talk or move much, but he has a big, friendly smile that draws everyone to him. "He responds with his eyes," his mother explains, "and makes little sounds" that convey his feelings to people who know him well. He manages to show when he is happy, and he is especially happy when his sister plays with him. Quiana helps dress Otis and entertains him when he is getting a bath or being fed. The children watch TV together and "she keeps him going. She flips and jumps and makes him laugh."

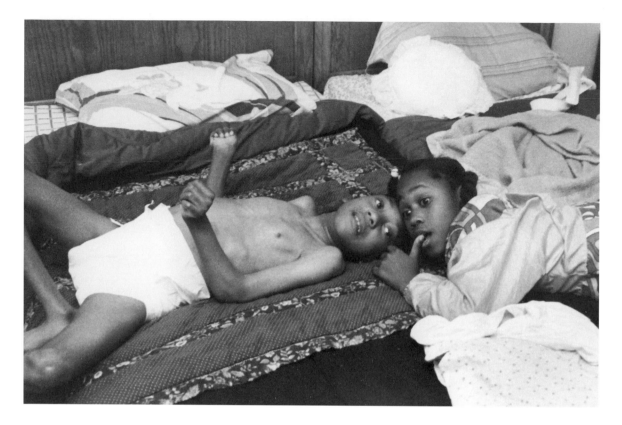

Otis has a full day at Berkeley High School. He is in a program for disabled children that offers physical exercises, special activities, and outings, along with academic subjects. He comes home at about the same time Quiana does, and after a snack they spend time together. Otis will watch Quiana play, or both children will watch TV or listen to music. Quiana is a shy child who seems happiest at home with her family.

Their mother knows from Otis' eyes that he understands what is going on. She can tell what he likes and dislikes, and she is "pretty sure he's smart, thinking-wise." She hopes that some day he will be able to get a communication device, like the one she recently read about that is being developed for people who are unable to speak.

The cause of cerebral palsy is unknown. Some people suspect birth injuries and blame it on the incompetence or carelessness of attending physicians. Like many parents of children with cerebral palsy, Otis' mother wonders about the doctor who delivered her son. She is not angry, she says, but "I used to get frustrated. Not anymore." Doctors told her that Otis would probably not live beyond the age of eight. But she trusted her intuition and learned everything she could. This, combined with her loving care, has helped Otis thrive. When Quiana was born prematurely, just as Otis had been, and with an even lower birthweight, "I didn't worry that she might be disabled; I was ready to accept and love her no matter what." She states with conviction, "If I had to start over again, I'd adopt a child with CP."

Most of the children's lives center around their many relatives. They only occasionally go to picnics or parties, but a multitude of aunts, uncles, and cousins are always around and give Otis a lot of attention. Otis may one day get a power wheelchair and other equipment that will make him more independent. It will be a matter of raising the money, his mother says, but she thinks the state will help pay for it. Maybe someday he will get a communication device so he can let his sister, his mother, and all his relatives know what he thinks and feels. They don't doubt that he feels their love for him—and that he loves them right back.

CASSIE

Cassie is eight. Her brother Martin is nine.

Cassie's brother Martin is her hero. She may not tell him in words, but it is clear from the way she tries to do everything he does—the way she imitates his actions and follows his lead when they play. Martin, a gentle boy, is not embarrassed by his sister's behavior or the fact that she has Down's syndrome. He is protective of Cassie and worries about her getting hurt at school. "Sometimes," their mother says, "he makes excuses for her when she needs to be scolded for bad behavior." Their parents watch Martin carefully to make sure that he isn't taking too much responsibility for his sister, which is something he is inclined to do.

Cassie and Martin have lived in the same neighborhood all their lives and have known their classmates and their families since nursery school. Both children are in an alternative public school that requires a considerable amount of parental participation. The other youngsters accept and know "the real Cassie," her father says, and the older children have organized "Cassie's buddies" to supervise her during recess. Although disabled children often go to special schools, Cassie's parents were determined that she go to an integrated school, and Martin was pleased to have her in the same school with him.

When Martin was three, his parents noticed that he seemed to avoid being close to Cassie. They encouraged him to talk about what he was feeling, and they discovered that he feared he might "catch" Down's syndrome from her. Since then, they have been very open with Martin and he is free to ask questions and express himself. He understands now that Down's syndrome is something "that makes her different. Nobody knows how it happened, but she can't do as many things as

I can." He is not particularly interested in explaining her condition to other kids, nor is he embarrassed by their reactions to her. If someone were to make fun of or say something mean about Cassie, "I would just walk away and tell an adult about it." When he is playing with his friends, Cassie can sometimes be a "brat," like any other little sister. "We just tell her to stop. But sometimes it's okay for her to be around because we're not really doing anything."

For Cassie, the main effect of Down's syndrome is that it slows her learning processes. While Martin can learn a new skill in only a few weeks, Cassie may take several years to reach the same point. "Whenever we think she can't learn something, she'll surprise us," their parents say. Cassie often accomplishes far more than anyone had expected. She will always need some help and supervision, but like her brother, she has an independent spirit and she will be able to take care of herself.

Her father's words are eloquent and moving as he describes what Cassie means to him. "Cassie is a teacher. She showed me another side of myself. She opened my life." He has learned to be open to people who are disabled or different, and to respond to the potential in others, not just to their appearance or superficial behavior. Cassie has helped her mother grow as well. Her mother recalls how it felt to see her infant daughter looking so lifeless in her crib. (Down's syndrome children have, among other problems, very poor muscle tone.) She remembers thinking, "I wanted a little girl, and here she is. Now I have a choice: either accept her and keep on living, or spend the rest of my life crying." Once she accepted Cassie, "I began to learn from her—there's a connection, a special communication."

Cassie has no trouble expressing her feelings with words and actions. She will tell Alana and Samantha, her best friends, "I like you a lot. I love you," or give a teacher or favored family friend a spontaneous hug. Cassie has recently discovered that marriage is something that is connected with love and family, so she asked Martin to marry her. Her parents have explained that marriage is between not a brother and a sister, but a man and a woman. Marriage means loving and being very best friends, too.

Her father points out with pride that "coming in contact with a child like Cassie helps people realize how much love a person can give and receive." Both Cassie and Martin are certainly bringing more love into the world.

ADAM

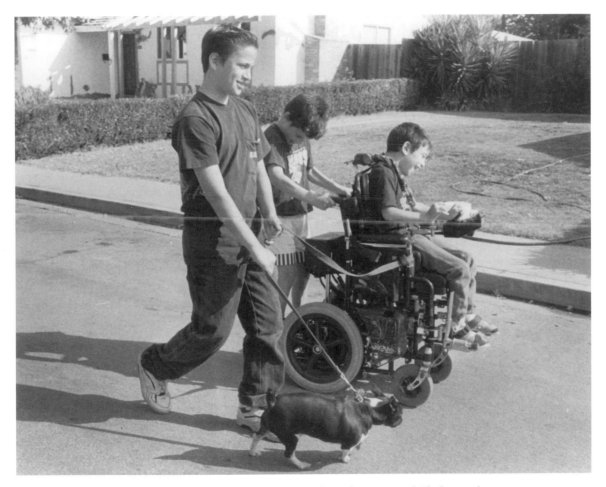

Adam is nine. His brothers are Jourdan, thirteen, and Skyler, eight.

I wanted a little brother and I got one," declares Jourdan, who was five when Adam was diagnosed with cerebral palsy. "I just got used to it. He was the little brother I wanted. I didn't care what happened to him as long as I had a little brother." It really wasn't as simple as he makes it sound. His mother recalls that Jourdan had to give up most of his activities after Adam's diagnosis. Adam required daily therapy and a great deal of special attention, which took an enormous amount of his parents' time and money. There was little of either left for Jourdan, though nobody remembers him complaining.

When Adam was an infant, he had minor physical problems that his parents might not even have noticed without Jourdan's normal development for comparison. It took nearly a year before a doctor gave them a definitive diagnosis, which they had more or less figured out for themselves. Then, when Adam was four, he had seizures that caused brain damage, resulting in serious learning disabilities.

Like most parents, Adam's parents had no experience with disability when he was born. They proceeded to study everything they could find on the subject. His mother became

an occupational therapist and has organized a resource and information sharing network to provide Adam with the best opportunities to develop. His father participates in his care as well, since Adam needs help with most of his daily activities.

Adam, who attends many types of therapy sessions, will probably always need help taking care of himself. Everyone in the family looks for ways to help him be more independent. Adam is friendly and cheerful most of the time and clearly enjoys his brothers' attention. His speech comes slowly and with difficulty, but he has ways of showing what he likes. He loves music, "especially loud rock and roll," his parents complain, and sometimes he pretends that he is playing a musical instrument.

Skyler is a year and a half younger than Adam. For Skyler, the family focus on Adam's development is the only way of life he knows, and he doesn't seem to give much thought to his brother's special circumstances. Skyler loves sports and outside activities. He doesn't pay much attention to Adam, except when he can ride around on the back of his wheelchair. Jourdan, on the other hand, spends more time with Adam and is sensitive to his needs and abilities. "I just play with him regular. Some things he likes to do regular, like any other kid, and some things he doesn't." He goes on to explain that "he can't do a lot of things that we can—walk and stuff. All he gets to do is watch movies and sit around."

Jourdan is a thoughtful youngster who knows exactly what he wants to do when he grows up: "Be an artist." At thirteen, he has already produced a number of paintings— he likes doing landscapes and works in acrylics—and is preparing for his first show. "Then maybe I'll get known for my art," he says modestly but with confidence.

Jourdan loves and accepts his little brother, and he is articulate in describing what Adam's disability means. "He likes going out. He doesn't get to do any of that. I used to think, before we had him, that kids in wheelchairs were lucky 'cause they didn't have to walk. But he wants to walk. He

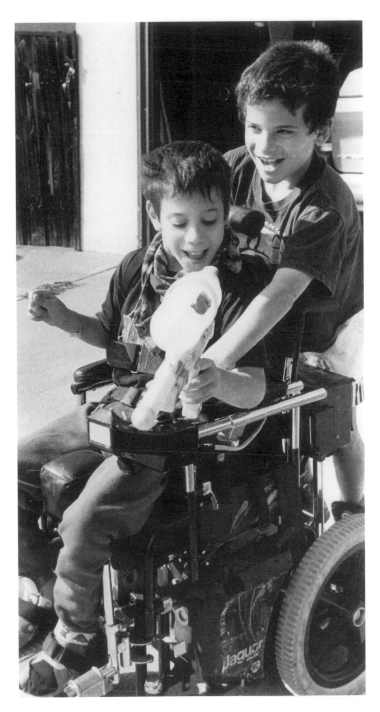

thinks it's really neat. When I was playing one day, he told Mom that he wanted to go outside and he wanted to chase me around and stuff like that. And it made me feel different about wanting to be in a wheelchair." When other kids suggest that Adam is lucky, Jourdan tells them that it's not like that. "I ask them, 'When you're on a long drive, do you like sitting the whole time and not being able to get up or stretch your legs or anything?' They'd say, 'No.' I say, 'That's what it's like, all the time. He can't walk.'"

Adam's parents are bitter about the pediatrician who insisted that they didn't need to worry about Adam and discouraged them from getting him into therapy when he was a baby. The doctor downplayed the seriousness of his disability, telling them, "He may not be a football player, but he'll be fine." Adam's father says sadly, "I'm sorry, but he's not going to be fine." It is true that with all his mental and physical disabilities, Adam is not "fine," but his warm smile shows that he knows that he is loved.

WALTER

Walter is fifteen. He has brothers Ron and Don, eight, and Rocky, five.

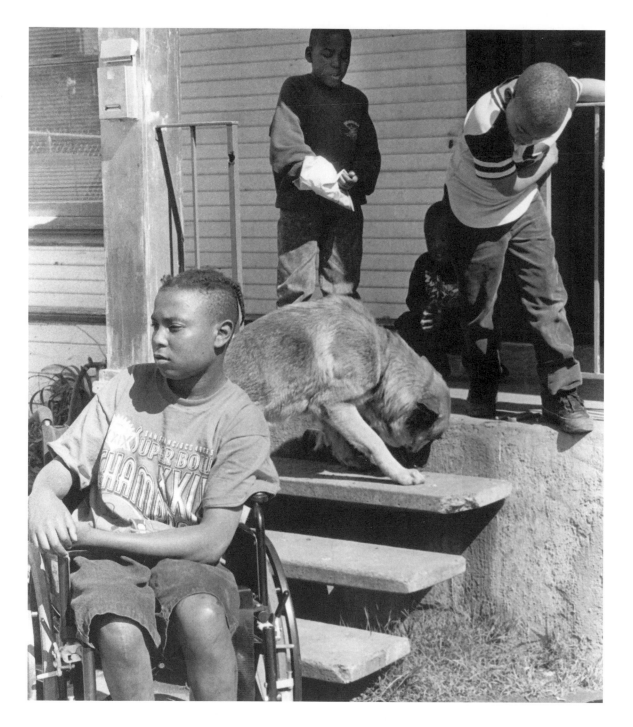

"Walter and his friend Tyson are our heroes," Walter's mother declares. His little brother agrees. "He saved me," Rocky says. "He pushed me out of the way so the car didn't hit me." The boys were putting air in their bicycle tires at a gas station near their home when a car careened into them. Thirteen-year-old Tyson was killed. Walter, who was fourteen at the time, sustained severe head injuries and numerous broken bones.

Walter was in a coma for a long time. He was moved from the emergency hospital to the children's hospital for rehabilitation, but the hospital discharged him three months later. He was making no progress, and there seemed to be nothing more that could be done to help him. At home, he lay in his bed or sat motionless in his wheelchair, responding to no one. The boys, especially the twins Ron and Don, were devastated to see their big brother so helpless. When he first came home, they were afraid to go near him. After a few days they got used to him, however, and wanted to do things for him. Their mother taught them how to put the formula into his feeding tube and encouraged them to help care for him. Although Walter did not talk and barely moved, Ron and Don and four-year-old Rocky continued to try drawing him out of his comatose state. When they left for school each day, they would go into his room to say goodbye. When they came home, they went straight to his room to let him know they were there and recount the day's happenings.

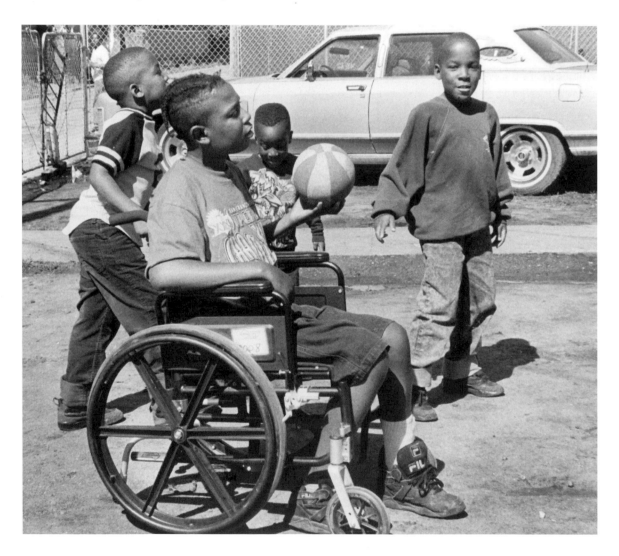

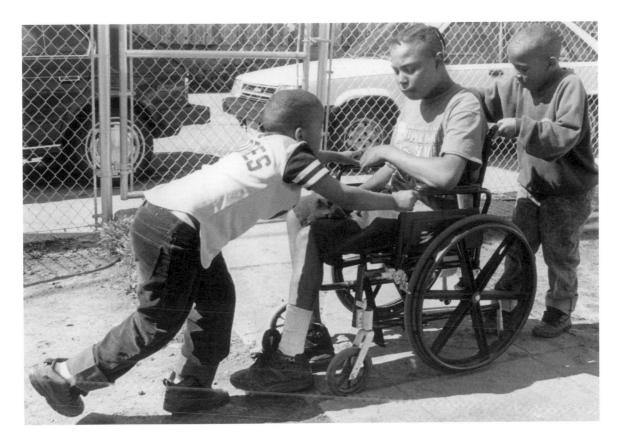

Four months after the accident, the extended family gathered to give Walter a fifteenth birthday party. His mother describes how Walter "woke up" that day. He was sitting passively in his wheelchair amidst the hubbub when his aunt focused on him and declared, "Walter, you gonna start communicating with me! Look at me," she demanded, "and follow me into the kitchen." At first there was no discernible reaction from Walter, but then it seemed that he moved his head ever so slightly. As the others watched, afraid that they might be imagining something they wanted so badly to see, his aunt moved around the room, all the while talking directly to Walter. And indeed, he moved his head and followed her with his eyes. Still not sure it was real, she began asking him simple questions requiring only yes or no answers. He responded by appropriately nodding or shaking his head. "That was the happiest day of my life," his mother says. "He was actually waking up."

A few weeks later, Walter was readmitted to the hospital for three more months of therapy. He came home for good just three weeks ago. He tires easily and gets grouchy, sometimes refusing to talk and rejecting help. Nevertheless, his brothers are ecstatic. Everyone is happy just having him home. "He's not totally Walter," their mother says, "but he's Walter. That's the most important thing to us—that Walter is with us again."

Remembering when Walter was hurt, Ron says, "I felt really terrible." He is still grappling with his feelings, wondering why it happened, if things could have been different. "I feel like it's my fault," he says. Then he bursts out, "I feel like it's Momma's fault for letting him go by himself." His mother explains that Walter was certainly old enough to go to the corner gas station by himself. "It's no one's fault," she tries to explain, "it was just an accident." Ron thinks about it for a moment. "I know whose fault it was, it's the driver's." "Don't you think the driver feels pretty bad?" his mother asks. Ron is not quite ready to accept that.

The twins complain that Walter likes their little brother Rocky the best. Walter lets Rocky play with his toys and go into his room. He even gave Rocky his remote control car. Ron wants to know why he gave it to Rocky, and Walter replies, "It's only one." Their mother interprets: "To give something to Ron and Don, he would have to have two. Besides, Walter figures that the twins have each other." But Walter lets them know that he loves them, too. There are occasions when he doesn't want his brothers to bother him, but Don admits that "sometimes he lets me lay down in his bed, and sometimes he even lets me wear his hats."

Walter hasn't returned to school yet and he is getting a little bored with having to stay at home. When asked what he would like to be doing right now, he answers, "Driving." He would like to drive an Oldsmobile Cutlass. That just happens to be his mother's car, and she teases him about thinking he is going to drive it. But what he wants to do the most, he says, is draw. Art has been his favorite subject in school, and he is determined to be an artist when he grows up.

Walter has a long way to go to heal from his injuries. What is even harder, is recovering from the trauma of learning that his best friend was killed in the accident that left him damaged but alive. He is fortunate to have three lively little brothers who don't mind telling him when they don't like what he's doing—and who don't mind telling him they love him and they are glad that he is their brother.

JoJo

*Jojo is three. His sisters are April, twelve, Allison, ten, Tiara, six,
and twins Jamie and Jillian, five. His brother Trey is one.*

Until seven months ago, Tommy—everyone calls him JoJo—was a normal two-year-old, walking, talking, and playing with his five older sisters and baby brother. But the family was troubled. His father had struggled with a drug habit on and off for years, but it kept getting worse. One day he went berserk and smashed JoJo's head with a baseball bat.

"He didn't do it out of hate or anger," their mother tries to explain to the children—and to herself. "He did it because he loved his son so much he figured, 'I'm going to die and I don't want to die alone. At least I'm going to take my baby with me.'"

The five-year-old twins were in the room and saw it happen. It is something they will never forget, especially since they were the ones to tell the police and doctors what happened. Since then, they have been going to therapy to help them remember that their father used to be kind and loving, and to understand that it was the drugs that turned him into a monster.

JoJo had fourteen hours of brain surgery and spent four months in the hospital relearning everything he had been able to do before. Although he is catching up to where he should be for his age, no one is sure if he will develop normally. His movements are still rather uncoordinated, and his speech is limited. His mother explains that "there's no predicting it. He may stop developing tomorrow."

It was impossible to guess how the children would react when they saw their terribly battered little brother. But they all dealt with it, and it brought them closer together. Before JoJo came home, nine-year-old Allison and her mother learned CPR and how to clean and replace the air tube in JoJo's trachea. When the tube gets plugged up, it has to be changed immediately because he can't breathe. The first time this happened was very frightening, his mother recalls. "I had to wake Allison up in the middle of the night to do it. Oh, gosh, we were shaking! But we did it." Allison is cool and casual now when she describes what it was like—how they had air bags and oxygen in case something went wrong when they were changing the tube. "I was really scared something was going to happen or that I would do it wrong or pull it out too hard. But then when I actually did it, I found out that it was really easy."

April remembers how she hated their father until she "found out what really happened." She continues, "I just thought he did it to hurt him, and I didn't know he was on drugs." She understands now what drugs do to a person, but it was difficult to accept. It was hard dealing with her own feelings, not to mention the prejudice and scorn of the community. "I'd go out and play with my friends and they knew what happened. They'd say the police and everybody knew more about it than my Mom did. And because of what happened they used to throw balls in my face and things like that." But she soon rejected those "friends" when she realized that she "didn't really care what they thought." What was important was when "we went to the hospital to see him, and I stayed and read stories to him and stuff. I was there when he first got to spend the night with us at the Family House. And then, when he came home, we were all happy." April is starting seventh grade now and making new friends. She says, "I still trust people. It's just that I've got to be a little more careful about who I trust."

Allison didn't encounter the prejudice and harassment her sister did. Her best friend knows about what happened, but she doesn't tell anybody and never brings it up with Allison.

The children's father was sentenced to eleven years in prison. Their mother admits that the lurid publicity around the case and the trial was difficult for all of them. But she hopes that other people who hear and read about the case will become especially vigilant when someone in their family is doing drugs.

JoJo is improving and the family has grown very close. But every day has been a struggle. JoJo's mother says "I never, never take for granted anything about my kids. I'd never take one day or one minute for granted that they're here, no matter how mad they make me or how happy they make me."

SOVON

Sovon is eight. His sister Logan is three.

When Sovon's mother learned that her son had cerebral palsy, she took it in stride. "You just deal with it, because you don't know anything else," she says. "He was my first baby and I didn't know what to expect. It was probably a good thing that I didn't know all you have to go through with a handicapped child." When Logan came along five years later, their mother took the same calm, accepting approach, allowing her daughter to learn by watching and figuring things out for herself.

Logan is a bright and lively child who seems to have an intuitive awareness and sensitivity about Sovon. She will say things like "Sovon can't walk but he's not a baby anymore," or "Sovon still wears diapers but I don't, 'cause he can't walk to the potty." Logan explains how she helped push his wheelchair "because he can't push." But there is a limit to how much they can play together and how much she can be trusted to do for him. Their parents worry that either of these two very active children might get hurt.

Sovon has a busy schedule. He has always gone to public schools where children with special needs are integrated as much as possible into regular activities. Unfortunately, the schools offering these programs change from year to year, "for the benefit of the child," his mother says with more than a hint of sarcasm. The transitions are difficult for Sovon, and there are always behavior problems for a month or two until he adjusts. "But there have been some very fine teachers who really care about the children and keep in close touch with the families," his mother reports, and Sovon seems to be thriving. After school he goes to a development center for disabled youngsters. During the summer he played basketball there and learned how to swim.

Logan is too young to help with Sovon's physical care, and the age difference limits how much they play together, but she has a positive effect on him nonetheless. Their parents have noticed that Sovon seems to pick up skills and concepts from her. Where he was once totally dependent on someone else to feed him, now he has learned to hold his spoon just by watching her. "He can turn the television off and on, he is aware of the remote control, and he knows what videotapes are. Logan makes him notice little things like that he just didn't pay attention to before," their mother notes.

In the family's inner-city neighborhood, Sovon hasn't had any real problems being accepted. Small children, his mother says, "will stand and stare and ask a million questions, but kids who know him are very patient and help him a lot." A thirteen-year-old neighbor boy "is here every morning to put Sovon on the bus. He's here every evening to get him off. He takes him outside, plays with him, takes him on walks." Getting Sovon in and out of the house is something of a task, since their second-floor apartment is at the top of a steep stairway. Nobody ever asked the boy to help, nor does he get paid for it. "He just does it." He seems to enjoy being with Sovon, who is a cheerful youngster, always ready to be on the go.

Sovon is bursting with energy. His inability to walk doesn't stop him from bouncing all over the house, nor does his speech impediment keep him from talking and making himself understood. Logan is no slouch, either. Their parents certainly have their hands full. But the children are happy; they play and fight like all siblings do. And for a few moments, Sovon sits quietly as Logan sings her favorite song: "I love you, you love me, we're a happy family. With a great big hug and a kiss from me to you, won't you say you love me, too?"

CHRIS

Christopher is fourteen. His brother Tony is seventeen and his sister Regina is twelve.

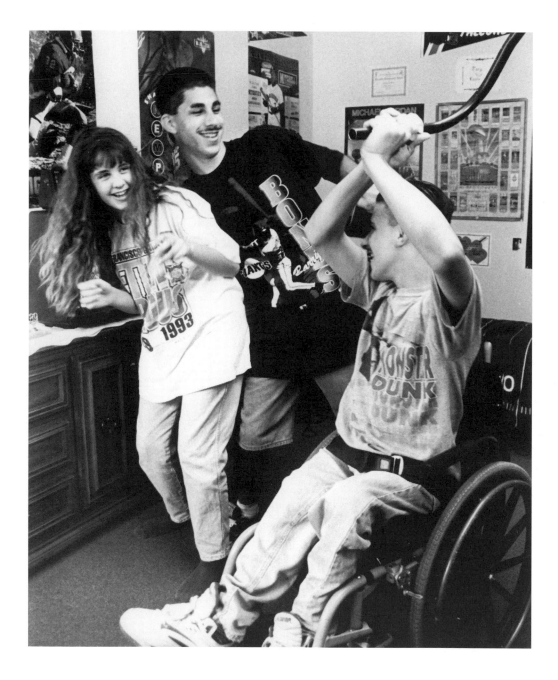

"Never give up is the first thing I learned," says Chris, who was the victim of an accidental shooting when he was seven years old. "When I was in the hospital, they would tell me to do things and I wouldn't. I thought there was no point because I wouldn't be able to walk." Chris is fourteen now. Although he has been through nine operations and years of therapy, he still can't walk, but he can do almost everything else. His big brother Tony urges him on: "Yeah. You've got to keep your head up. You know that you're a good person." Tony and Chris spend a lot of time together, working

out and playing ball or video games. Tony tells Chris, "You've got to do things, whatever it takes to keep healthy. You're still alive. That's the main point, you're alive." Chris's father is proud of how well he has recovered. "I think maybe it's the love that his mom and I and the kids give him as a whole family."

When the accident happened, Chris was staying at his aunt's house while his parents were away. He was playing outside and a boy invited him to his house. "I didn't ask my aunt if I could go to his house, but I went anyway. He said, 'I have a .22 rifle. Would you like to

see it?' I didn't know what to think, so I said 'Yeah, sure.' He got it out of the case and he said, 'It's not loaded. Would you like to hold it?' So I held it. And after that I gave it back to him. I looked away and the gun fired. It hit me in my arm, went through my stomach, and then hit me in the spinal cord. I tried to get up and I couldn't." The boy panicked, and

Chris was left by himself until the the boy's older brother found him.

Fortunately, Chris' father had insurance through his job, so the medical bills were taken care of. Their parents say, "We worried that Chris would have trouble getting around the house in a wheelchair. But many of our friends were willing to help us out." The next-door neighbor offered to move the property line to allow them an extra five feet to build an addition to the house. Materials and labor were donated, an architect drew plans free of charge, and Chris soon had a large room with exercise equipment as well as a specially adapted bathroom.

Tony, who was ten at the time of Chris's accident, vividly remembers how he felt when he heard about it. "I broke out in tears because they told me he wasn't going to be able to walk again. And that really hurt because, you know, I'm thinking we haven't really had a chance to do anything, like play on the same baseball team or go out and have fun together, because we were still young."

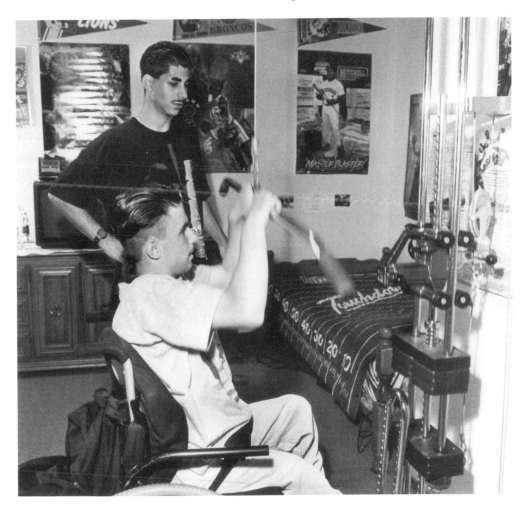

Gina was only five at the time of the accident and she, too, was upset. Even several years later, she burst into tears when classmates talked about a youngster who had been shot. Chris recalls how much his brother and sister helped him when he first came home from the hospital, getting things for him and helping him transfer in and out of his wheelchair. Now he is almost entirely independent. He can do all his own personal care, and needs only occasional help with transfers and putting his wheelchair into the van when they go somewhere.

Chris played baseball on a team for handicapped kids, while Tony played on a regular team. Each boy faithfully watched the other's games, and Tony also became a volunteer with the handicapped team. He remembers how, before the accident, he was unaware of what it means to be a handicapped person. Now, he says, "When I see a handicapped kid, I think, 'Wow, they're in a hard situation, because it's not easy.'" He realizes how hard it was for Chris, but he also shows pride as he describes how independent Chris has become. "Nobody has to hold his hand or anything. He does everything by himself. All we have to do is lift his wheelchair."

All three children are growing up, and their relationships and priorities are changing. Tony just graduated from high school and is busy with his job, his driver's license, and his girlfriend. Gina doesn't spend as much time with Chris as she used to, either. Her parents observe that "she's going from a little girl to a young lady. She's not in a good mood a lot." She often teases Chris and can make him very angry. Tony speaks up for Chris. "She will go in his room and grab his pillow or sit in his wheelchair. He hates that. He gets mad because that's just like his legs, you know." Tony is not above teasing Chris occasionally, too. But Chris can move quickly in his chair, and he will pull out his armrest and threaten to hit his tormentors with it. He has his own friends at school and in the neighborhood. His medical condition seems to be stable, and it looks like he will not need any more surgery.

For a time after the accident, the family was devastated. Tony says, "We were all crying 'it's not going to be the same anymore.'" But then they realized, "It's in our hands and we've got to deal with the cards that we've been dealt. We have to adapt to this." They have adapted—to Chris's disability and to all the changes that people handle in life. There are rough times, there are fights. But there is love and pride in each other, too.

MICHAEL

Michael is eight. He has sisters April, twelve, Theresa, six, and Tierra, five.
His brothers are Marcus, ten, and Terrence, three weeks.

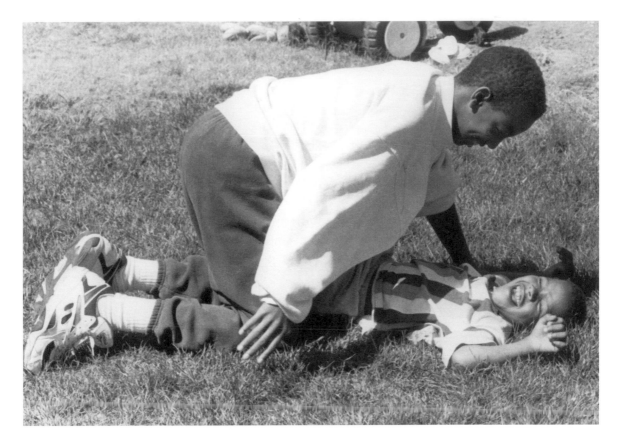

Michael lives at his grandparents' house, along with an older sister and brother and a host of cousins. Michael's accident happened two years ago on Labor Day, shortly after his sixth birthday. The children were playing in the backyard, and their grandfather was upstairs taking a bath. Michael's grandmother went shopping with Michael's cousin David. Michael didn't know that David had gone with his grandmother, and decided to look for him. He got on his bike and rode out into the street. At that moment, two cars came by. The first swerved and avoided him. The second hit him, tossing him and his bike across the street. He was badly hurt.

"We didn't think he was going to make it," his grandmother recalls. For three weeks he was in a coma. He had operations to repair his liver and kidneys and a tracheostomy so he could breathe. He lay on the bed without moving.

Two months later, he could breathe and talk on his own. He began to use a wheelchair and soon was playing baseball in the hospital corridors with his grandmother. When he came home for Christmas, he was beginning to pull himself upright. Two months later, he was walking again. Now the only thing anyone might notice is that Michael's left leg is shorter and his left foot drags as he walks or runs.

His passion for baseball and the encouragement of his huge extended family have helped him make an amazing recovery. Parents, grandparents, aunts and uncles, sisters and brothers, and dozens of cousins all came to see him in the hospital. Children under ten weren't allowed to visit patients in the wards, so everyone would gather in the cafeteria and the nurses would bring Michael down to join them. His cousin Ron was ten at the time and talks about seeing Michael when he first came out of the intensive care unit. "He was hooked up to a whole bunch of tubes, and everybody was scared to go in and see him. But I went in and asked the doctors questions about the tubes, and they told me about them," Ron asserts with pride. Michael's brother Marcus recollects that when he saw him in the hospital, Michael was in diapers. But that was only temporary, and Michael laughs about that now.

When he came home from the hospital, Michael was in a wheelchair and still pretty helpless. But there was always a raft of youngsters around who could absorb him into their play and give him help if he needed it without making an issue of his disability. "They were all there," his grandmother declares. "That's what helped him. He saw them walking, and he wanted to do what they did. He wanted to play ball like them. He'd get on his knees and pick up the bat, and they'd throw the ball to him and he'd hit it. That's what the therapist said kept him wanting to do more. So finally he decided that he was going to take a couple of steps. After that, it looked like it all came back to him."

With David pitching, others standing in the field or waiting their turn at bat, and Grandma cheering him on, Michael is at the plate with his unique stance, bat held ready. He swings, connects, and is on his way. His running is lopsided and his foot drags, but he keeps going. Nobody runs for him. He runs for himself, as he does almost everything for himself now. And maybe someday he will become the great baseball player that he always dreamed he would be.

ELIZABETH

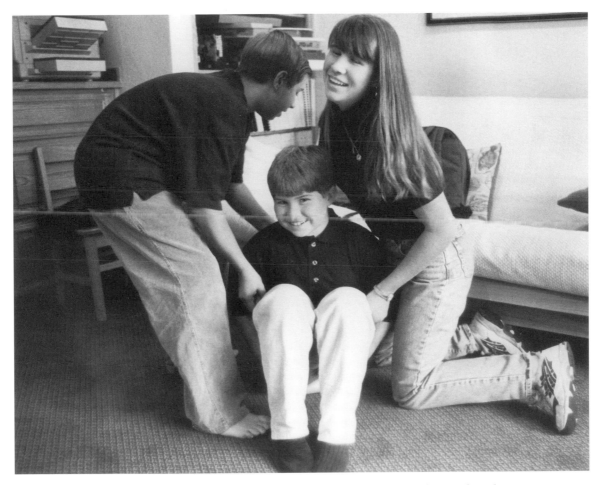

Elizabeth is fourteen. Her brothers are Andrew, eleven, and Daniel, eight.

Elizabeth's home is always neat and orderly. Nothing is left lying around where it might be tripped over by someone who can't see. "If we're not careful and Elizabeth hurts herself on something, we know we're going to be in trouble," says Danny. "Elizabeth gets real mad." Elizabeth, who is blind, wants to be independent and hates having to ask for help.

Her feeling about being blind is not so much anger as frustration. "It's the little, stupid things. Like I can't address an envelope, or I can't just look at the CDs and know what they are," she explains. She takes care of the CDs by marking them with labels she makes on her braille typewriter.

The boys don't mind helping Elizabeth. Danny is happy to lend a hand and appreciates it when she thanks him. She helps him, too, especially when he has difficult math problems for homework. Andrew sometimes acts as her "sighted guide." If they are walking together on a busy street, Elizabeth will hold his arm instead of using her cane. He likes doing that, but he feels embarrassed if she holds his hand instead of his arm. "People think that you're just dragging this person around," he explains.

How much help Elizabeth wants or needs from her brothers can be a problem. Andrew says, "once in a while she'll get mad at me and say that I'm trying to be parental." Elizabeth admits that she does occasionally get angry. "Sometimes I don't want to bother anybody. Sometimes when I ask for help, I feel stupid." But she appreciates her brothers' readiness to do things for her, and she knows that they are sensitive to how she feels about having to ask for help.

Another irritation for Elizabeth is the fact that she is the oldest child, and she knows the oldest is supposed to be more independent. Because of her disability, she can't always play the role that she feels she should play toward her brothers. "I get annoyed," she complains, "because the older sister is supposed to be more responsible. But they're more responsible for me, and they're younger." That is changing now that she is older. She is in charge of the boys when her parents go out. "She supervises them," her mother explains.

Elizabeth was not born blind. When she was six months old, she was shaken so violently by her nanny that she almost died. She was left with torn retinas in both eyes.

It took two years for the case to go through the court system. The sentence was a one hundred dollar fine, five years probation, and two thousand hours of community service. Elizabeth's mother tries to explain the rationale for the light sentence. "The court seemed to say, 'It wasn't like Elizabeth saw for very long, so she really wouldn't miss it.' They would have considered it worse if it had happened to an adult." Furthermore, the court encouraged the nanny to get a job, and nothing prevented her from going back to work taking care of other babies, in spite of the fact that she was a convicted child abuser. "That," says Elizabeth's mom, "really politicized me." Backed by the wholehearted support of Elizabeth's dad, she has been actively campaigning for legal reform.

Treatment of abusive child care providers has changed since then, and Elizabeth's family has had a lot to do with this. The state of California now has a registry of child care providers who have no history of child abuse. Elizabeth's mother expresses satisfaction knowing that "it is a way for another family to be sure they don't hire Elizabeth's perpetrator."

Elizabeth's family has also been instrumental in generating widespread public awareness of shaken baby syndrome. Such shaking is extremely violent and does not happen by accident. The whole family has appeared in public, on radio, and on television, educating people by telling their story. The children react differently at different times to being in the public eye. They are all outgoing and self-confident and realize the importance of their message, but sometimes they don't want to be in the limelight. Danny refused to appear on a TV interview recently because he was afraid his friends would think he was a show-off. Elizabeth declined an invitation to join her mother on a TV presentation, explaining that she had too much homework.

Their mother's activism taught the children to be independent at an early age. She spends long hours organizing campaigns, and is often away from home for public appearances and lectures. Their father also travels quite a bit. The children are able to fix their own meals and will do their homework without being reminded. Their parents appreciate Andrew for taking care of himself without complaining, and Daniel for his cheerfulness and always being able to make his mother smile. And they are certainly proud of Elizabeth.

All three children attend the local public schools. At a time when mainstreaming was not yet accepted policy, she was one of the first to be fully integrated. Her parents insisted on this, stating, "Elizabeth is a child who wants to be in the world; she's smart, she's social, she is who she is." She works hard and is an outstanding student with many friends. She complains that she doesn't get many invitations to her friends' homes, but her brother Andrew blames that on the fact that she is always studying.

Like many teenagers, Elizabeth feels that "my parents are overly protective. I'd like to go out more on my own." She has had a series of mobility teachers to help her learn the routes to the various places she wants to go. She recently walked alone to visit a friend in the neighborhood, and was outraged when her mother called to check if she had arrived safely. Elizabeth just turned fourteen and is determined to do everything for herself. "My main goal this year is to be really independent. My goal for my lifetime is that by the time I'm an adult, I can be as independent as a normal sighted person."

There is a lot of love and pride in this family. Andrew expresses it this way: "I'm proud of my sister because she gets straight A's, she's really good at school, and she sticks up for herself. She's just a really good sister."

ISHARA

Ishara is seven. Her sister Deshumbra is nine.

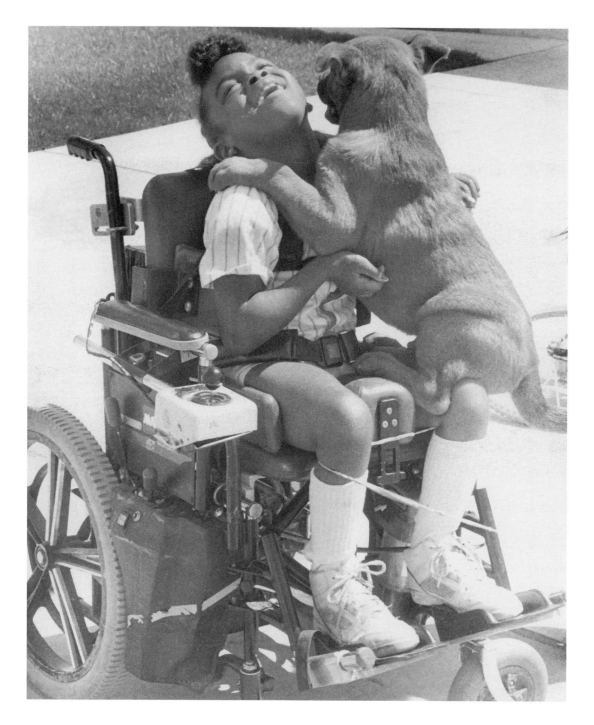

Ishara was eighteen months old and her sister Deshumbra was three when their mother put them down for their nap on an October afternoon. She needed some groceries, and the store was only a block away. Assuming that the girls were safely asleep, she dashed out. There is pain in her voice even now, six years later, as she talks about it. "When I came back, they had woken up and Ishara had fallen four stories from a window. It paralyzed her for life." Reconstructing the accident later, she guessed that they had gotten up and were playing on the couch, which was pushed up against a window. Apparently, Ishara fell backward and was hanging out the window while Deshumbra tried to hold on to her and pull her back inside. Deshumbra, a slender child, tried with all her might, but she couldn't hold on to Ishara.

The accident forced drastic changes in the family's life. Their mother was arrested for child endangerment, but she was soon released and put on probation. She immediately moved into the children's hospital, where she lived for the next year and a half. She was constantly at Ishara's side, seeing her through the intensive therapy that has helped her learn to do many things for herself. Deshumbra stayed with their father and accompanied him on daily visits to the hospital. Both the girls and their parents received counseling. This seemed especially helpful for Deshumbra, who felt guilty for failing to keep Ishara from slipping out of her hands. Deshumbra talks about the counselor. "She said, 'How do you feel?' and I told her, 'I feel upset.'" Asked if the counselor made her feel better, Ishara answers for her sister with a definite "yes!"

Their mother cannot forgive herself. "I still have guilt. I still cry, but not in front of the kids. I still blame myself." It is particularly painful when Ishara says, "I wish I could walk like the other kids. I wish I could play." Ishara has very limited physical function, but she has made tremendous progress. For example, she has learned to use wrist movements to get her thumb and forefinger together so she can grip objects. She wants to do things for herself, but she will always need a great deal of help. Her mother explains that the nerves controlling many muscles and internal organs are damaged. "She doesn't work well on the inside. She can't use the bathroom on her own. She can't cough on her own; she will choke, so you have to make her cough. She can't blow her nose." But she can feed herself and she is learning to dress herself. She is adept at controlling her power wheelchair.

Ishara, an exceptionally bright little girl, does not seem to have sustained any brain damage in the accident. She is in second grade in an integrated classroom in a regular public school. It is hard for her to write, so she uses a computer to do her homework. She already knows that she wants to be a singer when she grows up, and she definitely has musical talent. She also loves to move to rhythms as if she were dancing, although it is Deshumbra who plans to be a dancer.

Like sisters in any family, the girls have their fights. Their parents say, "They squabble over who gets to sleep on the big couch or who gets to sit in the front seat of the car and choose the radio station." But the girls love each other and play together with a host of friends and relatives. They are getting old enough to have chores around the house. Besides cleaning her room, Deshumbra loads and unloads the dishwasher. She also helps dress Ishara and fix her hair, but only when she "feels like it"—it is not one of her chores. Now their parents are trying to find appropriate tasks for Ishara to do. Deshumbra sometimes feels jealous of the extra attention that her sister gets, but their parents are careful to be fair to both girls. From time to time Deshumbra is allowed to spend a night at a friend's house, something Ishara can't do. Their mother declares that Deshumbra "sometimes needs a break. She needs to get away and she needs to know Ishara is not her responsibility." Ishara complains, with typical childish exaggeration, "She doesn't ever take me anywhere." However, when Deshumbra is away, her mother usually finds something special to do with Ishara.

"After the accident, the doctors, nurses, and social workers talked about putting Ishara in an institution." Her mother and father recall how angry they were at that suggestion. Now everyone is amazed at all the things the little girl can do. It took a lot of patience, work, and love. "But it's worth it," her mother affirms. "She is so independent and determined; it's amazing. We've really been blessed."